Equal Parts

by Kari Jenson Gold

STECK-VAUGHN
A Harcourt Company

www.steck-vaughn.com

A whole is made of many parts, parts that you can share.
There is a way to cut a whole so equal parts are fair.

A sandwich for lunch is fun to munch.
How can you cut this sandwich into two equal parts?

You can cut the sandwich in half.
That makes two equal parts.

$= \frac{1}{2}$

Here's a treat that you can eat.
How can you cut this cookie into three equal parts?

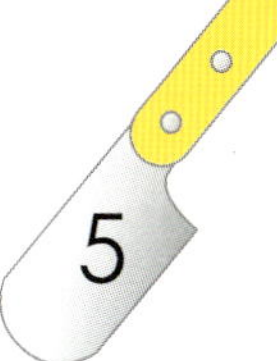

You can cut the cookie in thirds.
That makes three equal parts.

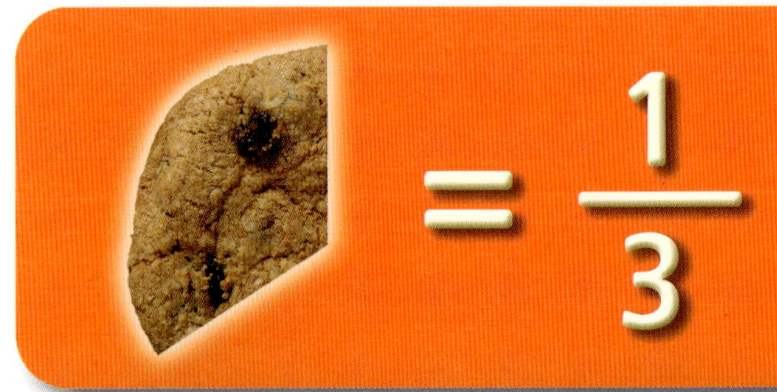

A melon that's sweet is fun to eat.
How can you cut this melon into four equal parts?

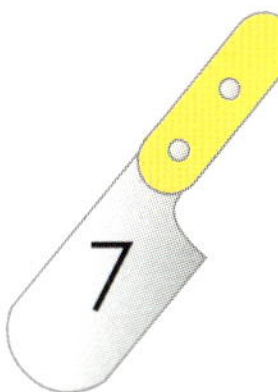

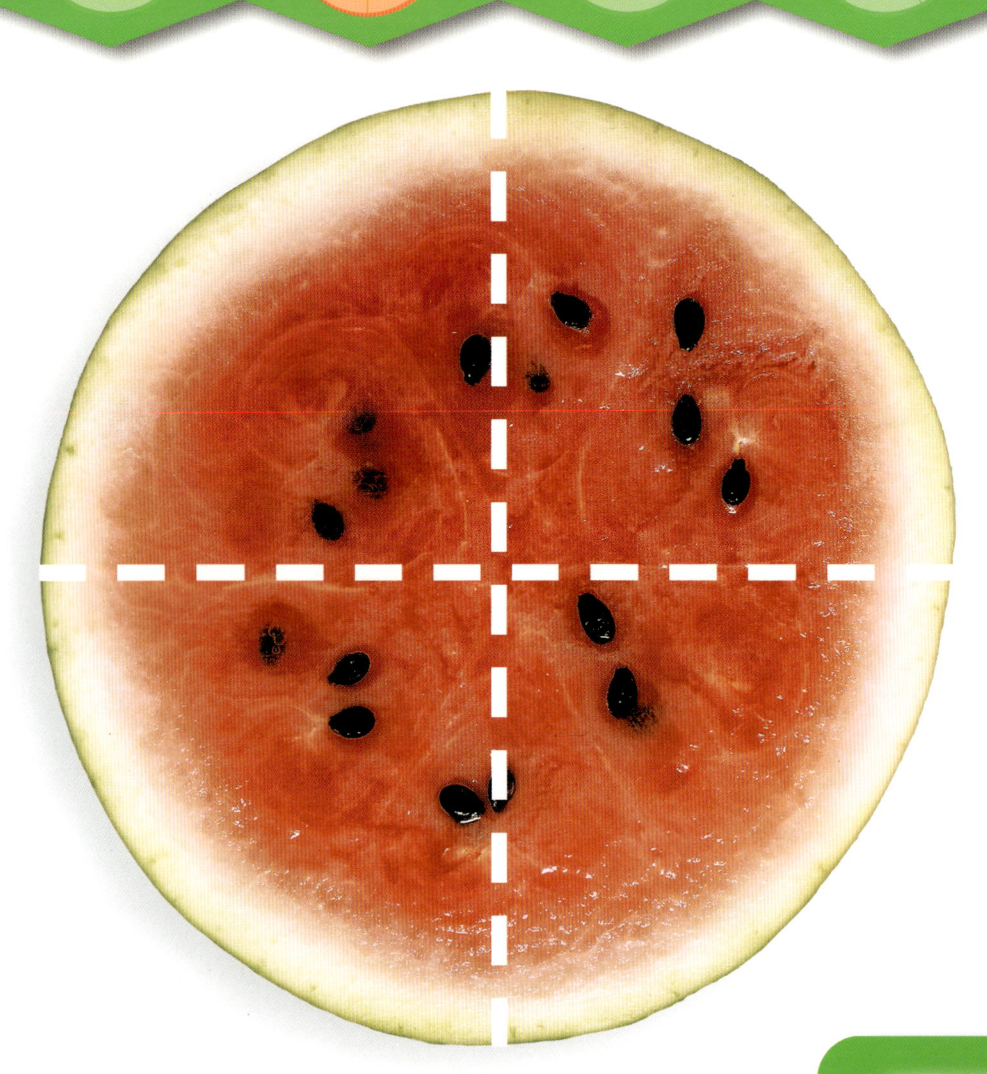

You can cut the melon in fourths.
That makes four equal parts.

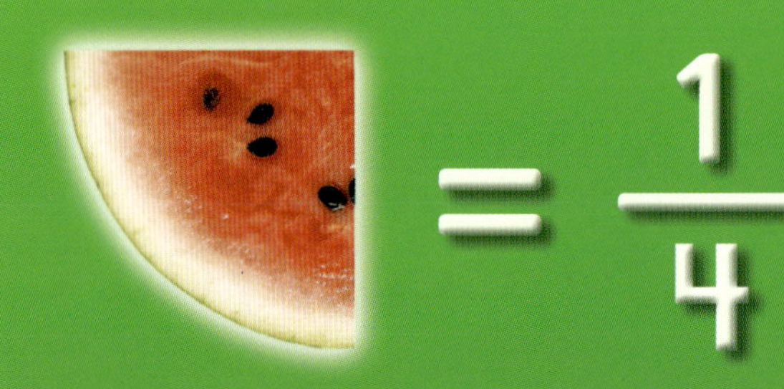

If you like to bake, try making a cake.
How can you cut this cake into five equal parts?

You can cut the cake in fifths.
That makes five equal parts.

It would really be so nice to share a pizza by the slice.
How can you cut this pizza into six equal parts?

You can cut the pizza in sixths.
That makes six equal parts.

Would you like to try a slice of fruit pie?
How can you cut this pie into seven equal parts?

You can cut the pie in sevenths.
That makes seven equal parts.

$= \frac{1}{7}$

A whole is made of many parts,
parts that you can share.

Halves, thirds, fourths, fifths.
Can you find them? Where?